HISTORY OF ROCK AND ROLL

The Roots of Rock
Volume II
1950's

Written by: Stuart Kallen
Edited by: Robert Italia

Published by Abdo & Daughters, 6537 Cecilia Circle, Bloomington, Minnesota 55435

Library bound edition distributed by Rockbottom Books, Pentagon Tower, P.O. Box 36036, Minneapolis, Minnesota 55435

Copyright© 1989 by Abdo Consulting Group, Inc., Pentagon Tower, P.O. Box 36036, Minneapolis, Minnesota 55435. International copyrights reserved in all countries. No part of this book may be reproduced in any form without written permission from the publisher. Printed in the United States.

Library of Congress Number: 89-84914   ISBN: 0-939179-73-3

Cover Photos by: Michael Ochs Archive
Illustrations by: Michael Ochs Archive

INTRODUCTION

If you traveled all over the world, everywhere you went there would be music. In every culture and in every country, people sing and play music. From the beginning of time, throughout all human history, we have entertained ourselves by dancing, playing musical instruments and singing. Music has helped the human race celebrate life together and has helped people understand each other better. Michael Jackson couldn't have said it better when he sang "We Are The World."

Many factors came together to give Rock-n-Roll its start. The invention of the phonograph made music available to everyone. When radio was invented, America was suddenly held together by a common thread, everyone listened to the same radio shows. With the introduction of television, people could see their favorite performers and imitate their looks and mannerisms.

After the hardships and sacrifice of World War II, America was enjoying riches and prosperity never before dreamed of. The Baby Boom added 76 million people to the U.S. population between 1946 and 1964. One of the side effects of this boom was the emergence of the teenager as a symbol for America. Teenagers walked differently, they talked differently, and most importantly, they had their own music. That music was Rock-n-Roll! Since Rock music is "people's music," this book focuses on the people who made it happen, when it happened and where it happened.

TURN YOUR RADIO ON!

A format of radio programming known as Top 40 was started in 1949, in Omaha, Nebraska, by a man named Todd Starz. Soon disc jockeys all over the country were playing the Top 40 hits. As a result the deejay became a very powerful person in the music business. Alan Freed was one such disc jockey. When Freed got bit by the Rock-n-Roll bug the world was never to be the same.

Disc jockey, Alan Freed, at radio station WINS in New York City.

ALAN FREED — THE MOONDOG

In 1950, Alan Freed was a disc jockey in Cleveland, Ohio. When Alan realized that many kids were dancing to Rhythm & Blues (R & B) records, he started spinning them on "The Moon Dog Show," his radio show on WJW. He called the music Rock-n-Roll, a term that was used in the 1947 R & B hit, "We're Gonna Rock, We're Gonna Roll," by Wild Bill Moore.

Alan Freed later moved to New York City and hosted a show on WINS. That show was breaking ground for many rock superstars of the 50's.

BILL HALEY AND THE COMETS — ROCK-N-ROLL'S FIRST #1 HIT

Bill Haley was born on June 6, 1925, in Highland Park, Michigan. He recorded "Rock Around the Clock" in 1954 and it was a moderate hit. One year later the song was used in the movie "The Blackboard Jungle," a movie about teenage rebellion. "Rock Around the Clock" then became a Rock-n-Roll anthem all over the country, soaring to number one on the Top 40. It was the first Rock song to achieve that position and paved the way for Rock-n-Roll's takeover of the Pop charts.

DATE DUE			
DEC 21 '94			
JAN 19 '95			
MAR 2			
APR 10 '96			

784.5
Kal

Kallen, Stuart A.

The roots of rock,
vol. II : 1950's.

17053

F.W. HOLBEIN SCHOOL LIBRARY
MOUNT HOLLY NJ 08060

394774 01294 55250B 05527E

ELVIS PRESLEY — THE KING OF ROCK

Elvis Presley was the first Rock-n-Roll giant. Presley's good looks and his great voice catapulted him from shy country boy to "The King" of Rock. No one in history had done what Elvis did in 1955. And to this day, years after his death, he is still considered "The King" by his many loyal fans.

BORN IN A SHOTGUN SHACK

Born January 6, 1935 in Tupelo, Mississippi, to Vernon and Gladys Presley, Elvis was one of a set of identical twins. His brother was still-born, leaving Elvis to grow up as the only child. The Presleys lived in the poorest section of town, near the railroad tracks in a "shotgun shack," so called because a person could shoot a shotgun through the front door and it would pass out the back door without hitting anything. So, Elvis Presley, who would one day become one of the richest entertainers in the world, was born in a family that had to struggle to meet the most basic necessities in life.

Elvis Presley, Rock-n-Roll's first "Giant."

IT STARTED IN CHURCH

Gladys and Vernon Presley went to church regularly. They took little Elvis with them whenever they attended the First Assembly of God Church on Adams Street in Tupelo.

Elvis' strongest memories of his childhood were of going to church. Elvis was sure that both the music and the actions of the preachers inspired his own singing and performing. This included his controversial stage movements, which caused a sensation after television appearances in 1956.

"During the singing," Elvis remembered, "the preachers used to cut up all over the place-that's how I was introduced to the onstage wiggle. The preachers did it. And the congregation loved it-why I even remember one day a preacher jumping up on the piano. I liked them, and I guess I learned a lot from them."

ELVIS GETS A JOB

When Elvis was thirteen, his family moved to Memphis, Tennessee hoping to improve their lot in life. Things actually got worse than ever, with the Presleys living in a cramped apartment in the poorest section of town. When Gladys got sick, Elvis was forced to take a job in the evenings at the Loew Palace, a movie theater. Elvis liked the movies, but failed at his job as an usher because he spent more time watching the movies than showing people to their seats.

Very few teachers or students remember much about Elvis until the last few months of his high school education. That's when Elvis changed his appearance quite radically. Suddenly he stood out from the crowd. While all the other boys had short crew cuts, Elvis grew his hair long, and had sideburns. He later said he did it because "that's how truck drivers wore theirs." Elvis wanted to be a truck driver just like his dad.

Elvis started wearing outrageous clothes that he bought at a store called Lansky Brothers, on Beale Street. Lansky sold clothes to entertainers, and their window was filled with bright and lively clothing such as pink sport coats and yellow jackets with leopard skin collars. "When he was seventeen, Elvis would come over and press his nose against the window like it was a candy store," recalls owner Bernard Lansky.

WHERE ELVIS LEARNED HIS CRAFT

Beale Street was also famous for blues clubs and street musicians. It was known as the "Home of the Blues." Black musicians came to Beale Street from all over, trying to earn some money for their families back home. Elvis lived one mile away from this musical melting pot, and was greatly influenced by the musicians who made Beale Street their home.

Music was becoming important to Elvis at this time and he spent many hours alone perfecting his singing and playing. He was surprised when a teacher at school entered him in a school concert, because he didn't think anyone knew he sang. He did so well at that concert that he had to come back for an encore!

Elvis left school in 1953 at a time when both his parents were ill and could barely stand to work. He got a job driving a truck for Crown Electric Company for $45 a week.

ELVIS MAKES HIS FIRST RECORD

While in Memphis, Elvis often drove by The Memphis Recording Service on Union Street. In that office was the Sun Recording Studio, owned by a man named Sam Phillips. For $4, anyone could make a 10-inch record.

On a Saturday afternoon in 1953, Elvis decided to make a record and give it to his mother for her birthday. Sam Phillips wasn't in, but his assistant Marion Keisker collected Elvis' four dollars and helped him record "That's When Your Heartaches Begin" and "My Happiness," a song that was made popular by the Ink Spots. Marion was impressed by Elvis. She made a tape recording of his songs and played them for her boss when he returned from lunch. Sam Phillips wasn't too impressed but told Marion to keep the young man's name and address on file.

ELVIS' BIG BREAK

Elvis returned to Sun on January 4, 1954, to record two more songs. Still, Phillips was not taken with Elvis' voice. Several months later when Phillips was looking for a singer to record one of his songs, he took Marion Keisker's suggestion and called "that singer with the sideburns."

Legend has it that Elvis arrived at the studio before Sam could hang up the phone. After recording several songs with terrible results, Sam

Elvis with his first band at Sun Studios, 1954. Scotty Moore on guitar and Bill Black on bass.

finally asked Elvis what he could sing. Elvis ran through his repertoire of Blues, Gospel and Country tunes, and finally-FINALLY! Phillips was impressed.

Phillips thought that Elvis had real talent but needed some other musicians to round out his sound. Two people who wanted to record for Sun were brought in-Scotty Moore, a guitarist, and his next door neighbor, Bill Black, who played upright bass.

In early July 1954, Elvis and his band went to the studio to try making some recordings. First a slow ballad called "I Love You Because" was taped, but it turned out badly. When the group took a break Elvis started clowning around.

Here's what happened next according to Scotty Moore:

"We were having Cokes and coffees, and all of a sudden Elvis started singing a song, jumping around and acting the fool, and then Bill picked up his bass and started acting the fool too, and then I started playing. Sam, I think had the door to the control booth open, I don't know, he was either editing some tapes or doing something-and he stuck his head out and said, 'What are you doing?' And we said, 'We don't know.' 'Well back up,' he says. 'Try to find a place to start and do it again.'"

What they were doing was the blues song "That's All Right" by one of Elvis' favorite musicians, Arthur "Big Boy" Crudup. But Elvis wasn't trying to copy the original song. He was singing it in a high, hurried manner, while Scotty and Bill played quickly to keep the fast tempo. It was the combination of white singer and black song that Sam had been looking for.

A few days later, Elvis was fooling around again, and did another favorite country song, this one "Blue Moon of Kentucky".

These two songs were released as Elvis' first record. It was exciting new music. It was Rock-n-Roll!

ELVIS HAS A HIT

A few days later "That's All Right" was played on WHBQ by Dewey Phillips. The name of Dewey's radio show was "Red, Hot and Blue" and it was certainly red hot that day. The phones started ringing at WHBQ as hundreds of people called the show to hear "That's All Right" again and again. Elvis' parents raced to the movie theater where Elvis was watching "High Noon" and dragged him to the radio station for an interview. When Elvis said that he went to Hume High School, it was then that the listeners realized for the first time that Elvis was white.

The record sold 20,000 copies in the Memphis area. At the same time Elvis started giving live concerts with Scotty and Bill, calling themselves the Blue Moon Boys. Elvis was known as the "Hillbilly Cat." The band had no plan at first, just to be better than anyone on the bill. The crowds got bigger and bigger.

Because Elvis was nervous, he moved around on stage. The more he moved around, the more excited the crowds got. At first he didn't know why the people were hollering. Then his manager told him, "The more you wiggle, the more they hollar." Girls had screamed at pop singers before, but no previous singer matched the reaction Elvis received.

Elvis released four more singles on Sun in 1955.

When Sun released the fifth single "Mystery Train" it was a number one Country hit.

The going was not always smooth or easy. When Elvis appeared at the Grand Ole Opry a stagehand told him he should go back to driving trucks. It took Presley weeks to get over it.

Fame took Elvis further and further away from home. Elvis was becoming a star, and staying away from home for weeks at a time. But he never forgot his parents. He called his mother every night before he went to sleep.

THE MAN WHO MADE ELVIS A STAR

Presley's continued fame and fortune had a lot to do with his meeting of Colonel Tom Parker. Parker was managing Hank Snow, the star of a country music package that Elvis was performing with. Presley was less known by the public than any of the other performers, but none of them, not even Hank Snow, were prepared to go on stage after Elvis got the crowd screaming and shouting.

Colonel Tom started booking Elvis for shows all over the South. Soon Parker had completely taken over Elvis' business affairs.

Parker also understood that if Elvis was to be successful some changes would have to be made. Sun Records had helped Elvis a lot but they were just a small record company. Parker approached many international record companies and asked for unheard sums of money for the singer's contract.

STARDOM AND A PINK CADILLAC

Steve Shoals at RCA offered Sam Phillips $35,000 for Elvis and all of his records made for Sun. No company had ever paid such a large amount of money for a new singer. Sam accepted because he needed the money to promote other singers on his label. Phillips believed there were many singers in the area who were just as good. When Carl Perkins, Jerry Lee Lewis and Johnny Cash had big hits with Sun, Sam felt justified in accepting the deal. Of course Elvis made untold millions for RCA, and as the years passed it became obvious that Phillips made a bad deal.

Elvis got a $5,000 bonus for signing with RCA and he bought his mother a pink Cadillac, even though she couldn't drive and had no drivers license.

ELVIS CHECKS IN-TO HEARTBREAK HOTEL

On January 10, 1956, two days after his twenty-first birthday, Elvis went to Nashville to make his first recordings for RCA. The band was made up of Scotty and Bill and D.J. Fontana, a drummer. Added to the band was Chet Atkins on guitar, pianist Floyd Cramer, and three male back-up singers known as the Jordanaires. All would work with Elvis on many more recordings.

"Heartbreak Hotel" was the first RCA release, and it became a number one hit around the world. The vocals were recorded in a stairwell at RCA giving them an echoing, booming sound. "Heartbreak Hotel" is still considered Elvis' finest recording.

Elvis was now breaking attendance records at all his concerts. Sometimes shows developed into riots. Red West, a childhood friend of Elvis', recalls: "Elvis was wearing a bright green jacket and black pegged pants. He leaned over the edge of the stage to kiss a girl's hand. She grabbed him and tore the sleeve off his jacket. That was the signal . . . The next thing there were girls on stage

Elvis, on stage.

and they seemed to go berserk. They were clawing like animals. Then his shirt was torn to shreds."

While Elvis was working the concert circuit, Colonel Tom was making better and bigger deals for Elvis. Television was the perfect place for him to be seen by millions of people. In 1956, Elvis appeared on many T.V. shows. This increased his popularity but also created controversy.

On the Milton Berle show, 40 million viewers tuned in to see Elvis. While singing "Hound Dog," Presley was gyrating madly to the music, while the girls in the theater screamed with delight. As a result, Elvis was panned in the press and shunned by the Ed Sullivan Show, the most popular show on T.V. This didn't stop Steve Allen from booking Elvis on his show, where he stood completely still and sang "Hound Dog" to a real live dog! The show was so successful that Ed Sullivan gave in and signed Elvis for $50,000 to appear on three shows. He sang to 54 million people. However, Elvis was shown only from the waist up.

ELVIS GOES HOLLYWOOD

In August of 1956, Elvis went to Hollywood to star in his first film, "Love Me Tender." It was the first of 33 Presley movies.

Elvis Presley's success had revolutionized the music business. Now, hundreds of radio stations were playing Rock-n-Roll. Buddy Holly summed it up best when he said, "Without Elvis, none of us could have made it."

The year 1957 ended with quite a sensation. On December 10, Elvis received his draft notice from the U.S. Army. He was to become a soldier on January 20, 1958. Elvis was proud to do his duty for the United States, and wanted to be treated like everybody else. Elvis Presley was transferred to West Germany and would spend the rest of the 50's doing his duty for Uncle Sam.

CHUCK BERRY
ROCK'S FIRST POET

"Hail, Hail Rock-n-Roll," "Long Live Rock-n-Roll." Perhaps no one has said it better than Rock's first poet and premier entertainer, Chuck Berry. With hit songs such as "Johnny B. Good," "Roll Over Beethoven" and "Maybellene," Chuck Berry has been credited for inspiring everyone from the Beatles to Bob Dylan to the Grateful Dead. Charles Edward Berry was born on October 18, 1926, in San Jose, California. His father, Henry, a carpenter, moved the family to St. Louis, and then a short time later to Wentzville, Missouri. Wentzville is a small town of 3,000 people, 50 miles from St. Louis. There, Chuck made his singing debut in the Antioch Baptist Church choir at the age of six.

St. Louis in the 50's was an exciting place for Black musicians. Chuck Berry joined the Johnny Johnson Trio and started playing regularly at many East St. Louis clubs. The Trio became a house band at the Cosmopolitan Club where they played for $14 a night. In May of 1955, Chuck went to Chicago where he met the legendary bluesman Muddy Waters. Muddy urged Chuck to audition for Leonard Chess, the man who owned Chess Records. Chuck played "Maybellene," "Wee Wee Hours" and "Roll Over Beethoven."

Leonard Chess liked what he heard, and pressed several "Demo" records to give to other people. A few weeks later Chess went to radio station WINS in New York City. Leonard then gave the

Chuck Berry doing the Duck Walk.

Demo of "Maybellene" to Alan Freed to play on his very popular radio show. The record wasn't even labeled with Chuck Berry's name yet. But, by the time Chess got back to Chicago, Freed had called a dozen times saying it was "his biggest record ever!"

MAYBELLENE, WHY CAN'T YOU BE TRUE?

By the end of July, "Maybellene" had climbed to the top of the charts. "Maybellene" would go on to become the first record ever to win Billboard magazine's "Triple Crown," entering the Pop, Country and R & B charts!

Chuck Berry was inventing a whole new language. "Cadillac cruisin' about 95/Bumper to bumper side by side . . . ," "Motorvating" over the hill . . ." - the first song about a guy, his car, and the woman that done him wrong! To quote Chuck Berry, "The man said, 'you got a hit, sign here,' and the rest is in the history books."

The following year would be one of hard work for Chuck Berry. On August 9, 1955, he played what he called his "first professional gig" in Chicago.

He then went on tour and played 101 shows in 101 nights!

Chuck was pushing ahead at top speed. Berry's band never saw much of him during those first tours because he was up in his hotel room everynight, writing more songs. Throughout the next year Berry released a string of singles whose influence is still felt all over the world. From the ripping guitar introduction of "Johnny B. Good" to the rock poetry of "Roll Over Beethoven," Chuck Berry changed the way the world played Rock-n-Roll.

THE DUCK WALK

He also changed the way the world looked at Rock-n-Roll. At the Labor Day show at Brooklyn's Paramount in 1956, Chuck Berry did his famous "duck walk." The move became a trademark for Chuck Berry, and it all happened by accident! As Chuck tells it, "I had to outfit my trio, the three of us, and I always remember the suits cost me $66, $22 a piece. We had to buy shoes and everything . . . anyway, when we got to New York, the suits, they were rayon but looked like searsucker by the time we got there . . . so we had one suit, we didn't know we were supposed to change. So we wanted to do something different, so I actually did that duck walk to hide the wrinkles in the suit — I got an ovation so I did it again, and again, and I'll probably do it again tonight."

When it comes to sheer creativity, wit and imagination, there are few people who could rival Chuck Berry. That is why his songs have been done by every major rock star of the past three decades. "Roll Over Beethoven" says it all:

"Well if you feel it 'n' like it/ then get your lover and reel and rock it/ roll it over and move on up/ just a trifle further and reel and rock it/ roll it over. Roll over Beethoven/ Dig those rhythm and blues. Woo!"

BUDDY HOLLY — ROCK'S TRAGIC HERO

"Something touched me deep inside/ The day the music died," sang Don McLean in his 1972 hit song "American Pie." The day McLean was referring to was February 3, 1959, the day Buddy Holly's chartered airplane crashed in a cornfield outside of Clear Lake, Iowa, killing Holly, Richie Valens and The Big Bopper (J.P. Richardson).

In the short span of three years Buddy Holly created a musical legacy that influenced everybody from the Beatles, to Bob Dylan to the Rolling Stones. No one knows what Buddy would have contributed if he had lived beyond his 22 years.

Charles Hardin Holly was born September 7, 1936 in Lubbock, Texas. His mother nicknamed him Buddy. At the age of eleven, Buddy began taking piano lessons. He had a natural talent for playing and after nine months he could play tricky Boogie-Woogie Blues riffs. Although he gave up his lessons after a short time, Buddy continued to play piano for the rest of his life. His main interest became guitar, and in the seventh grade he began playing and performing with Bob Montgomery, a friend also entering the seventh grade. Buddy and Bob were both influenced by Hank Williams, one of the most popular country musicians at the time. Their interests also ran toward Country music and Bluegrass.

Buddy Holly and band — "The Crickets."

THE BUDDY AND BOB SHOW

In September of 1953, the first full time Country music station in the United States began broadcasting from Lubbock, Texas. The new station, KDAV was started by "Hipockets" Duncan. The station had a Sunday afternoon show called "Sunday Party." KDAV announced that anyone who wished to perform should come down to the station that Sunday. Of course Buddy and Bob showed up and caught everyone's attention. Duncan, who also did booking and promotion of talent, could see right away that Buddy had the determination and grit to succeed. He encouraged the duo to add a bass player named Larry Welborn, and soon they were regular performers on the Sunday Party. Their thirty minute segment was called "The Buddy and Bob Show."

The show gave the team more exposure and they continued to grab whatever jobs came along. Buddy and Bob signed Duncan on as their manager, with the understanding that when they became successful enough to travel outside West Texas, Duncan would end his roll. Both sides knew that the boys expected to make a career of music and to become stars on stage and on record. When asked in later years, "At what age did you and Buddy decide that you wanted to be professional musicians?" Montgomery replied, "Oh, we always planned that, both of us. We never really considered anything else."

THE CRICKETS START SINGING

However, things did not work out at Decca, and by the end of 1956, Buddy was back in Lubbock, trying to put together a band. One day Buddy and his friend Jerry Allison were rehearsing. Buddy said, "Let's write a song." Jerry said, "That'll be the day." Buddy said, "Yeah, that sounds like a good idea." "That'll Be The Day" became the first hit for Buddy Holly and the Crickets on the Brunswick label, in the summer of 1957.

The Crickets were composed of Buddy Holly, Jerry Allison on drums, and sixteen year old Joe B. Mauldin, on stand-up bass. They did all of their early recording at Norman Petty's studio in Clovis, New Mexico. Norman was a musician who had started a recording studio, and was very helpful to Buddy, using his skill to polish the Crickets sound, and to get them a contract at Brunswick. He later became Buddy's manager.

"That'll Be The Day" was no overnight success. Six weeks passed before the record started to sell. But slowly the record caught on, and when it sold 50,000 copies, the Crickets got a telegram. The telegram was from Brunswick records congratulating them, and telling them to come to New York to begin a tour. At the end of July 1957, the Crickets flew east from Amarillo. The tour promoters thought the Crickets were a black group, and booked them on a week long, all black, package tour that played Washington D.C., Baltimore and New York. The Crickets joined another tour, billed as "The Biggest Show of Stars for '57." This tour featured Fats Domino, Chuck Berry, the Drifters, the Everly Brothers and more.

LIFE ON THE ROAD

This tour awakened the Crickets to life on the road. Although they were being paid $1000 a week, before expenses, the tour played for 80 nights, without one night off. The performers had to sleep on a bus during the long drives between cities. Then it was into the theater and on stage, usually for two shows, and then, back on the bus again for another five hundred mile ride. Tired, but too wound up to sleep, the musicians would pass the time with pillow fights, water fights, or maybe singing spirituals in the back of the bus. And people thought this was the glamorous life.

While the Crickets were on tour, Coral Records released "Peggy Sue" backed by "Everyday." That record, along with "That'll Be The Day," has sold over five million copies.

Buddy and the Crickets played The Ed Sullivan Show on December 1, 1957. Plans were then made for a tour of Australia and England. Their record sales were doing well in England. While they were there they had four records on the Top 30.

When the Crickets arrived back home, they immediately set out on another long tour. Buddy's schedule was so busy, he didn't even have time to do any recording. Fortunately, they had recorded two albums worth of songs before they became famous.

THE CRICKETS SPLIT

In the summer of 1958, Buddy was married to Maria Santiago. Maria was a receptionist for Peer-

Southern Music Co., Buddy's publishing company. It was love at first sight, but there were some problems with the marriage. Maria was from Puerto Rico, and at that time in America, mixed-race marriages were frowned upon. Buddy and Maria decided not to tell the press about their marriage, and it did not become public knowledge until after Buddy's death.

Things were changing for Buddy Holly. Now that he was married, he wanted to spend more time with his wife. This caused hard feelings with the Crickets. When Buddy decided to move to New York City and start a solo career, the Crickets and their manager, Norman Petty, stayed in Clovis, New Mexico. This was the end of the Crickets and the beginning of a new phase for Buddy.

THE DEATH OF BUDDY HOLLY

In early 1959, Buddy was asked to headline a tour billed as "The Winter Dance Party." This tour was to be a small one with just five acts. Most of the shows were to be in Minnesota, Wisconsin and Iowa. Buddy didn't want to do the tour, but his money supply was running out. Buddy also felt a loyalty to the promoters of the show because they had helped him out early in his career.

After rehearsing with a new band, Buddy Holly started his last tour. The Midwest was known for its energetic fans, and every small town had a ballroom where the crowds gathered to dance to Rock-n-Roll. The traveling conditions for the performers were dreadful. The first stop on the tour was Milwaukee, where the temperature was twenty-five degrees below zero! Things went from bad to worse. Bus travel was never comfortable, but now it was dangerous. The buses were poorly heated and had many breakdowns. Between Duluth, Minnesota and Green Bay, Wisconsin on the night of February 1, the tour bus died on a lonely road. The performers had to burn newspapers inside the bus to keep warm. After they were rescued by the police, the tour continued on to Clear Lake, Iowa. The tour arrived late on February 2, because once again, the tour bus was having mechanical problems.

Fifteen hundred teenagers came to see the Dance Party in Clear Lake that cold, windy night. The temperature was twenty below zero, as people filed into the Surf Ballroom. Admission was $1.25

each, and the crowd certainly got their money's worth.

The crowds went wild as Buddy took the stage. He sang "Peggy Sue," "That'll Be The Day," "Maybe Baby," "Rave On," and "Everyday." At one point a jam session took place with Buddy Holly, Ritchie Valens and The Big Bopper.

After the happy crowds had gone home, Buddy called his wife, Maria, in New York. He told her of the problems the tour had been having with the cold, dirty tour bus. Then Buddy told Maria that he was going to go ahead of the tour, to Moorhead, Minnesota, to take care of some arrangements for the next show. What Buddy did not tell Maria was that he was going to charter a small airplane to fly him to Moorhead that night.

Buddy Holly, Ritchie Valens and The Big Bopper arrived at the Mason City Airport at 12:40 A.M. After paying $36 each, the musicians boarded the Beechcraft Bonanza four seat airplane. Valens and The Bopper sat in back, while Buddy climbed in the front next to the twenty year old pilot, Roger Peterson.

Light snow was falling as the airplane took off at

1:00 A.M. on that cold and windy night. That was the last anyone would see of Buddy Holly. After the plane took off into the fog, people at the airport thought they saw it sinking off into the horizon, but they figured it was just an optical illusion. It was no illusion. The airplane carrying Buddy Holly, Ritchie Valens and the Big Bopper crashed in a corn field, killing rock's most promising musicians. The wreckage was not discovered until 9:30 the next morning. Everyone had died upon impact.

Although Buddy's life had a tragic ending, he still lives on in his music. Music that has brought great joy to millions of people, all over the world.

LITTLE RICHARD — THE FIREBALL OF ROCK-N-ROLL

"Awop bop-a-lop bop-a-wop bam boom!" So says Little Richard in the rock classic "Tutti Frutti." Born Richard Penniman in Macon, Georgia, Little Richard gave Rock-n-Roll its fire in the 50's. He sang with a frenzy and excitement that pushed Rock-n-Roll to its limit.

Little Richard, Rock-n-Roll's most original performer.

When Jerry Lee Lewis danced on his piano and pounded the keys with his foot, he was imitating Little Richard. When Elvis Presley swiveled his hips, he was imitating Little Richard. When the Beatles sang "Yeah, yeah, yeah," followed by "Whoo!" they were imitating Little Richard.

"Tutti Fruitti" was a hit in 1956, but not for Little Richard. The version that made it to the top of the charts was the version sung by Pat Boone. Pat was known as a "teen idol" because of his boy next door looks and non-threatening manner.

Little Richard had five songs on the R & B charts in 1956. The biggest one was "Long Tall Sally," a song Richard wrote about a girl from his home town.

The whirling dervish of Rock-n-Roll was too much for the white audiences of the fifties, and Little Richard had a hard time gaining acceptance.

Little Richards song's have become Rock standards, and he can be seen today on HBO specials and in many movies. The young man who once washed dishes in a bus station has come a long way.

JERRY LEE LEWIS — WHOLE LOTTA SHAKIN' GOIN' ON

On September 29, 1935, near Farriday, Louisiana, a child was born to Mary and Elmo Lewis. He was christened Jerry Lee Lewis, and he would grow up to shape musical history.

Jerry Lee tells how he got his start in the record business: "I read in a magazine about Elvis Presley, and Sam Phillips helping Elvis get started. I asked my daddy about it, and we collected — well, I should say, gathered all the eggs, for about three weeks, and we took the money and we went to Memphis, and I auditioned for Jack Clement, who worked for Sam Phillips at the time, and this is where I got my start. I cut 'Crazy Arms' and it stirred up a lot of noise, and we sold about 300,000 records of it."

Along with Roy Orbison, Carl Perkins and Johnny Cash, Jerry Lee Lewis was a member of the "Class of '56" at Sun Records. Of all the "rockabilly" stars at Sun, Jerry Lee was the wildest. This platinum blonde, piano pounding Rocker had the audience in a frenzy before the first words of "Whole Lotta Shakin'" escaped from his lips. He jumped up on the piano, played it with his boot heel, and shook his hair and screamed.

Jerry Lee Lewis, one of rock's wildest performers.

"A lot of noise" indeed. By the end of 1958 Jerry Lee Lewis was on top of the world. At the age of twenty-two he had sold over 20 million records, appeared as a guest star on eleven major T.V. shows, and had four gold records in a row.

Jerry Lee's career soon came tumbling down. In May of 1958 Jerry Lee flew to England to begin a 37 day tour. Flying with him was his new bride, Myra Brown. When the English press found out that Myra was fourteen years old, that she was Jerry's cousin, and that Jerry was still married to another woman, the tour was cancelled after only four days. Back in the states his records were being banned by radio stations all over the country, and Jerry's career ground to a halt. His career wouldn't recover until the mid-sixties, when he had a few minor country hits.

SAM COOKE — THE FOUNDING FATHER OF SOUL

The founding father of Soul Music was Sam Cooke. Sam was the first of the big Gospel stars to cross over to Pop music. Sam did this with great hesitation. Cooke was considered the most popular Gospel singer and his loyal audience considered Rock-n-Roll the "Devil's music." Sam's conversion to Pop sent shock waves through the Gospel and the Pop worlds.

Sam Cooke was born on January 2, 1931 in Clarksdale, Mississippi. The Cooke family moved to Chicago, Illinois when Sam's father, Charles, became the minister at the Church of Christ Holiness. When Sam was nine he joined his two sisters and a brother in a Gospel group called The Singing Children. When Cooke was in his teen years he joined a Gospel group called The Highway QC's, a group founded by R.B. Robinson, the baritone singer of a very popular group, The Soul Stirrers. Sam sang on the programs with all the nationally known Gospel groups who passed through Chicago.

THE SOUL STIRRER

In December of 1950, the lead singer of the Soul Stirrers quit the group. Suddenly, one of the most famous Gospel groups in the country was left without a lead singer. R.B. Robinson suggested the lead singer of The Highway QC's, a young

Soul Man, Sam Cooke.

man named Sam Cooke fill the spot. So at the age of twenty, Sam became the lead singer of a very well known Gospel group, a group known for its fine harmonies and rousing performances. The name Soul Stirrers says it all.

FROM SOUL MAN TO POP STAR

By the time 1956 rolled around, Rock-n-Roll was taking hold of America. It had been proven that the white audiences would buy records made by black artists. Ray Charles had hits with songs that were reworked from Gospel tunes. J.W. Alexander, Sam's promoter, decided it was time to have Cooke become a Pop star. Unfortunately, Art Rupe, the owner of Sam's label, "Specialty," was not convinced that Sam should cross over to Pop because he was afraid of offending the religious people. Art let his A & R man, Bumps Blackwell record Cooke to see what would happen. Sam recorded "Lovable," under the name Dale Cook, in 1957. The song was a Gospel song that The Soul Stirrers had recorded with the lyrics changed to make it a love song. "Lovable" sold 25,000 copies and so the experiment continued.

Art Rupe was still not happy with the arrangement and broke up a recording session one day when Sam was singing with a white female back-up singer. Rupe fired Sam and Blackwell and ripped up both their contracts. The recording session was taken down the street to Keen Records, a tiny label just starting up.

Keen Records released "You Send Me" in 1957, with the name Sam Cooke on the label. The song quickly went to number one on the R & B charts and the Pop charts. Cooke's beautiful treatment of "You Send Me" quickly earned him the title of "the greatest singer, ever."

Over the next few years Sam released a succession of hits such as "Only Sixteen," "Wonderful World," "Bring It On Home To Me" and "Another Saturday Night." These songs and many more of Sam's hits have been recorded by all the music greats over the years, and continue to be recorded to this day. Also worth noting is the fact that J.W. Alexander, Sam's promoter, started the first publishing company for black artists, Kags Music. This revolutionary move was financed by the huge sales of Sam's records.

A TRAGIC LIFE AND DEATH

Throughout his career Sam's life was marked by tragedy. In November of 1958, Cooke and singer Lou Rawls were seriously injured in an automobile accident that left Rawls in critical condition. One year later, Sam's first wife was killed in an auto accident outside of Fresno, California. In the summer of 1963, Cooke's youngest child drowned in the family swimming pool.

Then the ultimate tragedy happened to the honey-voiced singer from Chicago.

On the evening of December 10, 1964, Sam had an argument with a woman in his hotel room in Hollywood. The woman ran from the room, and Cooke thought she was in the hotel's main office. Sam pounded forcefully on the door of the office, scaring the night manager, Mrs. Bertha Franklin. When Cooke tried to force his way into the office, Mrs. Franklin pulled out a gun and shot him three times, killing him. She didn't even know she had shot one of the most famous black entertainers of the decade! It was a sad ending to a man known for his compassion and humor.

Over 200,000 people attended Sam Cooke's funeral to view the body. Many people didn't believe the official story of his death, and thought he was assassinated for challenging the white musical establishment. Whatever the case, there was an outpouring of grief that had been unmatched to that day. Every major black artist and many white ones attended the funeral, where Ray Charles and Bobby "Blue" Bland honored Sam Cooke in song.

In the end, there was almost no one who sang soul music who was not affected by Sam Cooke. Besides his inspiring singing and writing talents, Sam had a business savvy that led the way for black owned companies such as Motown. There are many entertainers today who are indebted to Sam Cooke's talents, and his music lives on.

FINAL WORD

Time and space does not allow the mentioning of all the thousands of people who have shaped Rock-n-Roll. Some made untold millions of dollars and are known the world over, some are nameless and known to only a few. From its humble beginnings to the multi-billion dollar music industry of today, Rock has always owed its success to the common people, the people who sang and danced and "Let It Rock."